POWHER SIMPLICITY

A Woman's Guide to Crypto Confidence

SONYA MEADOWS

(Founder of PowHer Token)

ISBN: 979-8-9952412-0-1 (paperback)

To every woman who was never taught about money but expected to survive without it.

To every woman who learned strength before security.

To every woman choosing knowledge over fear.

This book is for you.

Preface

From Confusion to Clarity

Crypto used to feel like a language spoken too fast and explained too little.

I watched women nod along in conversations they didn't fully understand — not because they weren't smart, but because the information wasn't being shared with care, patience, or protection.

This book exists to change that.

PowHer Simplicity was written to teach cryptocurrency in plain language — without intimidation, without pressure, and without shame. You do not need a finance background. You do not need to be technical. You do not need permission.

You need understanding.

Crypto is not just about money. It's about access, ownership, protection, and choice. When women understand how money moves, we stop surviving systems that were never built for us — and we start building our own.

By the end of this book, you will:

- Understand what crypto actually is
- Know how blockchain works
- Protect yourself from scams and rug pulls
- Know what to look for in white papers
- Understand wallets, exchanges, and ownership
- Build confidence to invest wisely
- Move forward without fear

This is not about hype.

This is about empowerment.

Welcome to the future of money — explained with clarity, care, and PowHer.

— Sonya

Table of Contents

Chapter 1

The Currency of Sisterhood

Money is energy. It flows through relationships, opportunities, communities, and decisions.

For generations, women have been expected to manage households, raise families, and stretch resources — without being taught how money actually works. Cryptocurrency changes that.

Crypto is simply a new way value moves — one that removes gatekeepers and gives women direct access to ownership. No approval. No judgment. No waiting.

When women understand money, families change.
When women understand crypto, legacies change.

This book is not about becoming rich overnight. It's about becoming informed, protected, and confident in a world that is already shifting.

You belong in this conversation.

Chapter 2

What Is Crypto, Really?

Cryptocurrency is digital money secured by powerful code.

It is not fake.

It is not imaginary.

It is not a trend.

Crypto allows you to send, receive, and store value digitally — without banks controlling the process.

Crypto is:

- Global
- Fast
- Transparent
- Secure
- Permissionless

Anyone with a phone and internet access can participate. Crypto doesn't ask about your background, your credit score, or your past mistakes. It only recognizes your wallet address.

That alone makes it revolutionary for women.

Chapter 3

Centralized vs. Decentralized

Understanding this chapter means understanding why crypto exists.

Centralized systems are controlled by institutions — banks, payment apps, and corporations. They can freeze accounts, reverse transactions, and change rules without notice.

Decentralized systems are controlled by the network — not a single authority. You control your wallet. You control your funds. No one can block or freeze your assets.

Centralized means permission.
Decentralized means freedom.

Chapter 4

The PowHer of the Blockchain

Blockchain is a permanent digital ledger — like a diary that everyone can see, but no one can erase.

Each transaction is recorded, verified, and locked in place. Once written, it cannot be changed. This creates trust without needing a middleman.

Blockchain protects truth.
Blockchain protects transparency.
Blockchain protects ownership.

This is why crypto works.

Chapter 5

Crypto Wallets: Your Digital Purse

A crypto wallet does not store money — it stores access.

Your crypto lives on the blockchain. Your wallet holds the keys that allow you to move it.

There are two main types:

- Hot wallets (online) for everyday use
- Cold wallets (offline) for long-term protection

A smart woman uses both.

Your wallet is your responsibility. Protect it like you would protect your identity.

Chapter 6

Private Keys & Seed Phrases

This is the most important safety chapter in the book.

Your private key and seed phrase control your wallet. Anyone who has them owns your crypto.

Never:

- Screenshot them
- Store them digitally
- Share them with anyone
- Enter them into websites

Write them down. Store them securely. Treat them like the keys to your future.

Chapter 7

Staying Safe: Scams, Hackers & Rug Pulls

Crypto creates freedom — but freedom requires awareness.

COMMON SCAMS INCLUDE:

- Fake customer support
- Guaranteed returns
- Fake airdrops
- Romance scams
- Pressure tactics

RUG PULLS

A rug pull happens when a project builds hype, collects money, then disappears.

Red flags:

- Anonymous teams
- No white paper

- No roadmap
- Hype without purpose
- Founders holding most tokens

HOW TO KNOW IF A CRYPTO IS A GOOD INVESTMENT — WHITE PAPER CHECKLIST

A white paper is a project's blueprint.

Look for:

1. A real problem being solved
2. A clear roadmap
3. A visible, experienced team
4. Fair token distribution
5. Real utility

Good projects educate.
Bad projects pressure.

Chapter 8

Exchanges: Where You Buy & Sell Crypto

A crypto exchange is where you purchase cryptocurrency using traditional money like U.S. dollars.

Think of an exchange like a store.

There are two main types of exchanges, and understanding the difference is critical.

CENTRALIZED EXCHANGES (CEX)

Examples:

- Coinbase
- Crypto.com
- Binance

These platforms:

- Require identification

- Are beginner-friendly
- Allow you to buy crypto with a debit card or bank account

However, when your crypto stays on a centralized exchange, you do not fully control it.

That's why there's a common saying in crypto:

Not your keys, not your coins.

Smart women buy crypto on an exchange — then move it into their own wallet.

DECENTRALIZED EXCHANGES (DEX)

Examples:

- Uniswap
- PancakeSwap

DEX platforms:

- Do not require ID
- Connect directly to your wallet
- Allow peer-to-peer trading

You keep control of your crypto at all times.

SMART STRATEGY

Buy on a centralized exchange.

Store and manage through your wallet.

Trade on decentralized exchanges when ready.

Chapter 9

Tokens, NFTs, and Nodes

Crypto is more than coins — it's an ecosystem.

COINS VS. TOKENS

- Coins operate on their own blockchain (Bitcoin, Ethereum).
- Tokens are built on existing blockchains (PowHer Token on Ethereum).

Both can hold value — the difference is structure.

NFTS (NON-FUNGIBLE TOKENS)

NFTs represent digital ownership.

They can be:

- Art
- Music
- Membership access
- Event tickets

- Educational passes

NFTs prove authenticity and ownership on the blockchain.

NODES

Nodes help operate blockchain networks.

In return, node operators may earn:

- Ongoing rewards
- Passive income
- Long-term value

Think of nodes as digital infrastructure — not hype.

Always research before investing in node projects.

Chapter 10

The PowHer Token Ecosystem

owHer Token was created with intention — not hype. It exists to:

- Educate women financially
- Promote transparency
- Support community wealth
- Encourage generational ownership

PowHer is built on three pillars:

1. Education
2. Community
3. Legacy

This ecosystem is about women building together — safely, intentionally, and with knowledge.

Chapter 11

Building Wealth the Smart Way

Wealth is built through:

- Patience
- Consistency
- Education
- Emotional control

Crypto is not a casino.

SMART WEALTH RULES

- Invest gradually
- Research before buying
- Avoid emotional decisions
- Take profits strategically
- Diversify investments

Slow, steady growth outlasts hype every time.

Chapter 12

The Future Is Female & Decentralized

The future of money is already here.

Women now have:

- Direct ownership
- Global access
- Financial independence
- Protection from gatekeepers

Crypto allows women to:

- Protect wealth
- Transfer value freely
- Teach future generations
- Break cycles of financial dependency

Decentralization gives women choice — and choice is power.

Author's Note

If you've ever felt intimidated by money conversations, let this book be proof that understanding is possible.

You don't need permission to build wealth.

You don't need validation to protect your future.

You learned.

You grew.

You stepped forward.

That alone changes everything.

— Miracle

PowHer Glossary

Simple Crypto Terms

Blockchain — Permanent digital ledger
Crypto — Digital money secured by code
Wallet — Stores access keys to crypto
Private Key — Secret access code
Seed Phrase — 12–24 recovery words
CEX — Centralized exchange
DEX — Decentralized exchange
NFT — Digital proof of ownership
Token — Asset built on a blockchain
Volatility — Price movement up/down

THE POWHER PLEDGE

I commit to learning before investing.
I protect my wallet and my wisdom.
I move with clarity and intention.
I build wealth without fear.
I honor my future and my legacy.

PowHer Refresher Quiz

Multiple Choice

1. **What is cryptocurrency?**
    A. Government-issued cash
    B. Digital money secured by code
    C. A video game reward
    D. A bank coupon

2. **What does decentralized mean?**
    A. Bank-controlled
    B. Company-controlled
    C. User-controlled
    D. Unusable

3. **What is a blockchain?**
    A. Social media platform
    B. Permanent digital ledger
    C. Password manager
    D. Website

4. **Where do you BUY crypto?**
    A. Wallet
    B. Exchange
    C. Email

D. Bank vault

5. **Where do you OWN crypto?**
    A. Exchange
    B. Wallet
    C. Bank
    D. Website

6. **What is a seed phrase?**
    A. Password nickname
    B. Wallet recovery words
    C. Discount code
    D. PIN number

7. **Should you share your seed phrase?**
    A. Yes
    B. Sometimes
    C. Only with support
    D. Never

8. **What is a rug pull?**
    A. Market correction
    B. Project scam where creators disappear
    C. Price dip
    D. Crypto reward

9. **What is a white paper?**
    A. Advertisement
    B. Project blueprint
    C. Receipt
    D. Coupon

10. Smart crypto investing requires:
     A. Gambling
     B. Hype
     C. Long-term strategy
     D. Guessing

Answer Key

1 — B
2 — C
3 — B
4 — B
5 — B
6 — B
7 — D
8 — B
9 — B
10 — C